Google

Classroom

A Step-by-Step Guide that Will Allow You to Master the Transition from the Physical Classroom to the Digital Classroom with a Simple and Clear Method

Jones Miller

Table of Contents

Introduction

Google Classroom is a free online tool Google developed for schools to allow development, distribution, and task rating easier. The crucial purpose of Google Classroom is simply to streamline a platform through which learners and teachers share knowledge. Google Classroom is estimated to recruit between forty to a hundred million individuals. The key purpose of Google Classroom is to provide such a platform by which students and teachers share data digitally in total privacy of their rights. Google Classroom makes more effective and practical teaching by streamlining activities, strengthening collaboration, and promoting communication. Google Classroom integrates the presentations, forums, emails, data, and calendar into a common platform for student-teacher interaction. Students may be invited to join a class or imported automatically from the school domain, with a unique code. Google's environment allows teachers to send, create, and mark assignments all indoors. The class generates the specific folder in the individual's drive, which students will submit to the instructor to credit their work. Attributions and due dates are included in Google's Calendar; each task may also belong to a subject or group. Teachers may monitor the progress for each pupil by evaluating the revision background of a text, and after grading, teachers can even return the research along with feedback. Google Classroom is built for teachers to enable them to save a lot of time, organize and arrange classes, and enhances the overall contact between teachers and students.

Educators are able to construct courses, carry out tasks, submit reviews, and see everything in one place. The Classroom often easily combines with other Google tools, with such simple configuration. Teachers can schedule a lecture, allowing students and other teachers to participate. They will share information about the assignments, questions, and resources on the Classwork tab. Google Classroom saves paper and money. An instructor establishes courses, distributes tasks, meets, and remains structured in one location. Better preparation. The tasks should appear on the To-do list, on the class calendar, or in the class stream. All class components that are put into directories can move instantly. Gs-tract and reins are increased. It will create tasks, submit alerts, and automatically launch classroom discussions. Students communicate and connect with each other via e-mail or also in the class stream. It's practically easy to use Google Classroom, anybody with a Google account will be able to use Google Classroom. Organizations that use G Suite for Education, non-profits, schools, independent educators, home school children, administrators, and families are all eligible to use Google Classroom. Teachers and students are key participants, who may use a school account to use Google Classroom.

Teachers can also quickly assess who achieved or missed the topic and can give direct real-time feedback and scores. This function works with the many software that you have. The classroom requires work on to be done on Google Docs, Gmail, Mail, Drive, and Forms. It is easily accessible and user friendly. It's available to colleges, to individuals, to charities. This often does not contain advertisements and is only used for rating purposes through content or student info. Google describes Google Classroom as "The school retracts ammo," so this might be the easiest way to think about it. Putting Google G Suite resonates as a forum for teachers and students alike. It also acts as a digital hub where teachers can store learning materials and share them with students on time or schedule for another time—many of them paperless. You can pick what features you want to incorporate in there. This is easy, and in seamless imitation of the popular Google imps, is probably what has rendered Google Classroom one of the most frequently used apps of today.

Chapter 1: What is Google Classroom?

Google Classroom is like a finer learning system. Google for Education is a vital set of resources to connect across the schooling cycle; one of the services is Google Classroom, which is really user friendly. Google Classroom is free; Google built an educational resource for classrooms. This aims to create paperless tasks, to automate, disseminate, and analyze them. The online service provides Google Drive for data creation and preservation; Google Docs for reporting, Sheets and Photos, Gmail for communications, Google's scheduling, and the task job calendar. Students can be admitted to the Classroom by their specific application or automatically imported from the school domain. Within the corresponding user path, every class will create a separate folder. iOS apps are accessible for iOS and Android smartphones, enabling people to capture photos and add them to assignments, sharing Google Classroom enables teachers to build an electronic interactive learning environment where they can access all the documentation their students need. Documents are saved on Google Drive and can be updated in software, such as Google Docs, Sheets, etc. Google is more different in the classroom, unlike any other e-learning school. The most valuable aspect of Google Classroom is the simple way teachers and students will interact.

1.1 Teaching Online in Moments of Crisis

This emerging pandemic has led to the closure of schools around the world, taking close to one billion children worldwide out of school. As a consequence, the program radically changed with the distinctive advent of e-learning, where multimedia and on digital networks teaching is performed. Research demonstrates that online learning has been shown to enhance the transmission of information, so it requires less time to say the problem may take longer to go away. While nations are at differing points of a global pandemic rate, there are currently over 1.0 billion children in several countries worldwide affected by school disruptions related to the pandemic. In Denmark, children up to the age of 11 return to nurseries and schools following their initial closing on March 12 but in South Korea, electronic students respond to their teachers' roll calls.

For this sudden step away from the traditional classroom in some parts of the globe, the doubt is whether there will continue to be post-pandemic tolerance of online schooling and how such a transition would impact the global education market. Everything is emerging as the current pandemic is impacting citizens all over the world, particularly healthcare and educational institutions. Schools were among the first places to be taken down in nations like the United Kingdom, and, as a consequence, as the pandemic progressed, Google Classroom achieved attention across the globe.

For students sitting at home and teachers searching for ways to pass out homework online, Google Classroom has become the go-to alternative. The classroom is available to most pupils, which allows instructors to communicate with their whole group at different levels. Since the outbreak ended, Google's classroom has seen usage grow to over 100 million user's overtime. That number was mentioned last week during the announcement to incorporate Google Meet Classroom. The growth of Google Meet itself, which amid the outbreak had 25x more use in March, is also remarkable since it launched in January. Bloomberg was able to include a little insight behind the scenes for the production of Google Classroom too. Google's VP in control of G-Suite said he received an email from his European colleagues in March with a question from Italy's education minister wondering whether Google's app will push the whole country's school system online instantly. "Several sleepless days and nights" later, Italy's system for millions of children was up and running. During the following years, Google Classroom expanded further in other nations. With Google's vice president for education, Indonesia has seen comparable growth with that of Italy, saying both of these places have been lighting up over the last month. Google has made remarkable success. Unfortunately, it reflects the epidemic's ramp-up and distribution. Google has always seen a very clear presence in the education market with services, such as Classroom and Chromebooks, but the pandemic epidemic will only solidify the position.

Chapter 2: Getting Started With Google Classroom

Google Classroom is a program that lets teachers monitor their students' learning processes. Teachers can create a class within the platform, provide an add-on code to their students or email them, and quickly begin interacting with students about class details, assignments, and documents.

Google Classroom is a perfect way to introduce students to ways of finding knowledge and of communicating/collaborating digitally in a secure and readily available, self-contained space. Google Classroom should be implemented in primary school and should be used to complete in middle and high school. Recent research shows that while working on assignments, Google Classroom greatly increases the students' accessibility of materials and collaboration.

More than likely, you do have a Google account, and G Suite for Education has been recorded with the school system IT administrator. When the system hasn't been enrolled yet, the organization must be licensed by a school official and the employees and students must establish a Google account. This person would also need to make sure the Google Classroom is turned on and include you as an instructor to build courses.

2.1 A Brief Introduction

Google Classroom's great aspect is that it's self-contained, so that even those in the jurisdiction have access to it, and it provides a degree of protection for school-age children. On the other hand, regardless of the privacy laws, you'll note that you cannot share your classroom with anyone in the school jurisdiction. Guardians, if this choice is switched on, will provide email summaries of their student advancement. Google Classroom integrates the other apps as part of the Google Apps for Education collection to include a more streamlined learning environment. Google Classroom is a free, paperless online tool developed by Google for Schools to ease task formation, distribution, and grading. Google Classroom's primary objective is to streamline the process of teacher-student file-sharing. Google Classroom is a program that is only open to schools with Google Applications enabled for Education or Non-Profit Accounts Google Software. Google's Classroom contains Cloud Drive for job development and delivery, Google Documents, Composition Sheets, and images, Communications, Gmail, and Schedule Google Calendar. Students may be invited to enter a particular class using a hidden code or imported from a school domain automatically. Google Classroom generates a different folder on the drive of the corresponding person, in which the student may respond to the teacher concerning a task. Mobile apps, available on iOS and Android devices, let users take snapshots and connect to assignments, exchange links with different ape communities, and offline awns details. Teachers should monitor each pupil's development, and teachers should return to the job with input after graduation.

Google Classroom is a free resource for teachers that are collaborating with students. Professors may create an online classroom to welcome students to the class, then build and delegate assignments to them. Google Classroom allows teachers to build an online class and handle information for their students as a whole. Files are saved on Google Drive, which can be accessed in Google Docs apps. However, what is distinct from Google's regular classroom, Google Drive experience is the Google-developed student-instructor framework for students and teachers to think and function. Students and teachers will explore the tasks inside the Google Classroom, and teachers will monitor the student's success. The schools will use Google Apps for Education to register for a free Classroom account.

The core characteristics in the Google Classroom are the students and instructors that have links to apps not included in Google's accounts under the School software. For example, teachers can add images in forms to questions or respond to multiple choices. Inbox by Gmail has classroom messages clustered in the mailbox, which makes it easy for teachers and students to discover relevant information and highlights. The school tool often lets teachers coordinate learning streams by attaching topics to texts, so teachers and students may scan for specific topics in the flow. Google Classroom also fosters interaction with friends. Teachers are welcoming and guardian too. Summaries of student work and automatic updates of student work and class notices in the Google Classroom.

Google Classroom assists in accessing data from other apps and offline processing knowledge. Teachers may monitor each student's success, and with added feedback or extra tasks, they can return the work after marking. Released in 2014, Google Classroom became immediately popular, mainly because of its speed, ease of use, and performance. In 2017, was accessible to everyone to encourage every specific Google user to access the classes without needing to have a G Suite that is registered by the district for Educational account, and all personal Google users were eligible to build and perform classes in April of the same year. In 2018, Google introduced a curriculum redesign, introducing a segment in the classroom, updating the grading system, enabling the sharing of classrooms from other schools, and implementing tools to support teachers organize.

Before you use Google Classroom, there are a couple of things you should learn. Therefore, you will not use them for the wrong motives.

It's a forum for online learning, so it's not:

- **A test or quiz tool**: if you want to make quizzes with Google Classroom, there are some possibilities, but it is still not meant to be a quiz tool on its own. In the end, there are so many nice apps. Think about quizzes for Google Forms or Book Widgets.

- **A private message case**: while you are working with Google Classroom you can make an observation on assignments and announcements, but no private message function is available. If you wish, you can give them an email to stay in constant touch with your students, or you can enable other Google educational applications to replace this feature.

   In Google Classroom, you can incorporate assessments and tasks from other educational applications, such as a Book Widgets exam, which is automatically assessed.

- **Within Google Classroom itself**: include a query. So pick a transparent reply or a query with multiple choices. Nonetheless, this feature is not that inspiring. To make your Google Classroom a better choice so you should take the first choice.

- **A debate forum**: you might give updates, so students will vote about them, although it is a perfect conversation environment. You may look into Padlet if you're considering a basic but powerful, free classroom resource that will promote conversation among students.

Chapter 3: What Does Google Classroom Do?

Google Classroom is immersive learning software that can be used for educators and learners on the internet or any computer. This offers a digital forum for better organization and streamlining of professional learning. It is composed of four parts, each with distinctive features and purposes.

- Stream

- Classwork

- People

- Settings

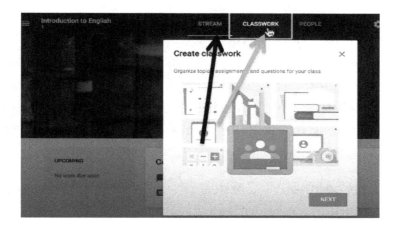

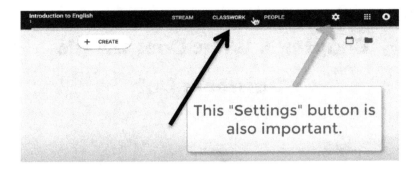

This "Settings" button is also important.

3.1 Segments

Google Classroom provides a live "Class Stream" where teachers can make major announcements and students can see what tasks have been made. This is the way to go for educators. Messages or exchange details in a connection, photo, or document format.

Under the "Classwork" titled page, teachers should give assignments or quizzes, exchanging lesson content or posing the class a question.

The "People" titled page include the teacher's name and a number of all students involved in the class. That's where you'd go to send an email to a student or guardian, as well as check to see what assignments a particular student has input by writing to their name.

The segment "Grades," which is for instructor accounts only, offers a simple and convenient system for awarding grades to students for and assignment you make.

The software also creates Drive files automatically for any task, teacher, and learner. This useful app includes a single repository for all your Classroom information, including the multimedia resources that you exchanged, each project that was produced, and the student research that was done. It helps you to keep focused and free up time, so you can work on more meaningful stuff.

Google Classroom lies between you and Google Drive and provides a teacher / student-friendly way to handle documentation in classrooms. Here's what Google Classroom can do for you:

- **Taking up assignments**: the most critical thing you do in Google Classroom as an instructor is to build homework tasks for your pupils. While planning an assignment you will upload the materials required for students to read or operate on. Students are told of the new assignment through e-mail. Once completed, the students will 'check-in' the duties and then rate the assignments. Google Classroom lets you build a special class for each class you are teaching. You can build a class in only three steps.

The classrooms are divided into multiple parts:

o In the Student section, you may also decide if the students are given permission to focus on the queries, updates, and tasks you are making, or whether they should only do so. Alternatively, you can choose to not permit students to comment or to comment in the classroom on posts.

o You'll find the posted questions, announcement, and another discussion you create in the Stream section. It is the area you'll be spending much of the time after setting up the courses. Further discussed is about Google Classroom assignments, questions, and announcements.

o All the students in Google Classroom can be seen in the "Students" section. Students can be added by inviting them or by giving them a code on the left side of the screen while creating the class or you can use your account on Google to let your students join your class. Tell the class code to your students whom you want to enter. Students sign into their Google Accounts from their phones, tablets, or Chromebooks and use the class code to enter.

- **Making assignments**: the first thing you'll do in Google Classroom as an instructor is to making homework tasks for your pupils. You will upload the appropriate information for the students to read or report on while making a post. Students are told of new assignments via e-mail. Once the tasks are done the students "turn in," and you will then rate the tasks. Google Classroom Assignments is the best feature. You can attach files while submitting work. You can connect any files from your device, a Google Drive file, a video from YouTube, or a connection to any internet site. Teachers can also share any news on the internet or device with their students in an instant.

- **Any file of any sort can be attached by students on Google Classroom**. Students can submit their work in folders, but teachers can also access and rate them without any delay. Teachers can always count on getting the assignments submitted by their students and grade them as well, as soon as they want.

- You can, as a teacher, for example, give an essay to your students and they can turn in their finished essays from any device that has an Internet link to the task you generated in Classroom. Teachers can check the files at school or home and store it on their computer. Printed assignments are no longer required as they can be submitted directly to Google Classroom. This paperless assignment submission works well both for the students and teachers as they do not have to waste time.

- **Make announcements**: If you have a short message for the whole class, you can easily type in the notification that is delivered via e-mail to all the classmates.

- **Store materials for classroom use**: the materials you add to your assignment are not the only documents you can store. Google Drive allows you to store any other necessary documents for students.

- **Allow students to interact**: students can comment on assignments and announcements and email each other via the Classroom interface.

- **School supplies for Google Classroom**: you can further store any other not related documents in different folders in Google Classroom. For students, you can store any other necessary documents on Google Drive.

- Enable students to interact: Students can comment on tasks and announcements as well as send an email to each other via the Classroom GUI. Your students must, of course, be able to share comments. Why don't they? That is entirely up to you! You are the Google Classroom supervisor.

  Google Classroom can manage permissions, allowing the students to talk, just report, or just only allow the instructor to control that, just comment. And the students will be e-mailed separately.

- **Google Classroom helps you to make updates, in addition to making tasks and queries**. Announcements can be replied to or acknowledged, by developing a chain, you may answer back. The whole student body should have one announcement-based discussion. Teachers also have the choice to attach a notification script, a video, or a connection.

- **Good place to receive updates**. Google Classroom can also send reminders to the students of the dates of assignment due. You may also submit updates right now or can be scheduled for later, this will help you and your students keep focused.

- **If you have a class that requires a ton of commercials, so it is feasible to think those homeroom teachers would use the commercial option to post**. The list continues on and on, notes, approval papers for any matter. Students would not be able to lose them.

3.2 Customizable Grading Scheme

Teachers may pick a grading method and build divisions of grades. If teachers wish students to have exposure to the total ratings or teachers can pick from below mentioned systems:

- **100% points grading**: distribute all points received by the students by being divided by the highest possible grades.

- **Weighted by class grading**: weight is allocated to grade levels. For the grading to be out of 100% it is necessary to average to combine average of all categories.

- Whether teachers chose not to rate the pupils

at all, let them complete their work without assigning any points.

- **E-Discussions**: teachers may invite students to answer questions and answer classmates. Comments on Google Docs make for a two-way conversation, because teachers may give students feedback; it is a fantastic way to keep students interested, particularly when they are not seen. Teachers will control the conversations by opting to silence from announcing or posting on certain particular students.

- **Advertisements**: teachers can provide announcements to update the students. Advertisements are posts with no homework assignments to them; they're just student notices; about when to submit the assignments or tests in class. Teachers will plan notifications when to post them later and monitor the announcement responses made by the students or co-teachers.

- **Google classes live**: one of the best features of Google Classroom is in which teachers can virtually take a live class via Google Meet. Teachers can connect with more than 200 participants on this platform, which can live-stream about more than 90000 viewers. It is also important to capture such meetings or lectures so that students who skipped the live session can revisit them. For later, it can be watched by those students who missed the live lecture.

3.3 Setting up Google Classroom

Like most mobile applications, you need to use a Google account. But not any single Google account will do for Classroom; you need Google Apps to account for education. This is different from your Google account as a standard. To set up, one obey the measures below

1. Ensure that the school is listed with the G-Suite in the Educational sector.

2. You can read all about the program on the Google Apps for Education website, or only click the "Get Apps Today" button in the upper right corner.

3. Fill out your institutional information on the form and click on the "Next" one.

4. The school would most definitely have a web portal, so you'll want to access it. Use the domain name you already have purchased, click

the domain name option and type it.

5. Go to classroom.google.com on a web browser. You're expected to sign in with a Google account.

6. Type the username you want to use and the password.

7. In the image, type the requested text to show that you are not a computer, test the "Read-and-Agree" tab, "Allow," and sign on.

8. To build classes, you would require instructor control and connect your students to a classroom.

9. If you use a regular Google account you will see a message saying "Sorry! Classroom is accessible for school applications only on Google Apps at this period." Then click and begin the Applications.

10. Next, add the students by adding them to the "People" tab. The students were all brought into the school domain by the Google system administrator for quick access for you to connect to the classroom.

11. When entering their email you will INVITE the students (If the school has community sharing, their name can show in the box when

you enter their password.) The students can head to http:/classroom.google.com then click on the "+" sign and choose the option "join the class."

Google builds your database and signs in to the administration server. You'll have to validate the domain from there, which suggests you'll have to show that you "own" to it. If you are using the domain of your school, on that step, you will need the help of your Webmaster.

3.4 Timing-Saving Elements of Google Classroom Include

Photocopies: instead of trying to produce fresh papers for each learner, you will render a Google Docs replica of only one for each learner in your class, with just one press away.

- **Task and grade management**: this software helps you to easily and effectively delegate due dates for each project and return grades. You do have the choice of having no due date, so students can take their time without any strain. If you've completed a task, you will submit it to the recipient, enabling them to access their score directly, as well as any written reviews you have provided.

Check which students have completed their assignment at a glance by clicking on the assignment's link. It will inform you of the number of students who sent it in and who are losing their work. You may also go to segment "people" and after clicking on the name of the individual student to see which assignments they have been assigned, and what work they have completed.

- **Direct reviews**: to provide prompt input directly on exchanged papers and posts. There is also an option to leave a comment on any assignment that has been turned in so that you can give positive praise for a job well done or give tips for corrections that are needed.

Chapter 4: Step-by-Step Guide to Understanding Google Classroom

Google Classroom was built to focus on consuming less time, resources and more on instructional energy, and it has certainly measured up to the advertising.

The app has simplified the process in the classroom and is allowing contact between teachers and students simpler. Google Classroom does a few items at its heart and does them well.

o It creates a central home for educational activities.

o It lets educators create assignments, posts, and announcements from any internet device (and other class activities).

o It collects assignments from students.

o It helps teachers to grade assignments and provides feedback.

o It returns graded assignments to students.

Before you start with Google Classroom, make

sure you are signed in to your Google account. Click on setting and try to find Google Classroom there:

1. Go to google.com

Google Classroom is now available for both Google for Education and regular Gmail accounts. Anyone who has a Google account now can use Google Classroom.

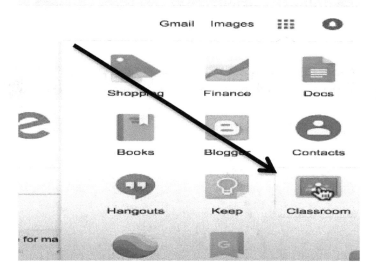

2. To build the first folder, press the "+" button at the top-right.

(Next to the checkerboard icon you are using to access all your apps) Then click on "Create class."

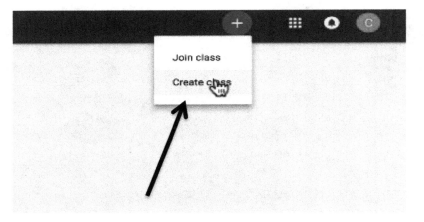

If you start for the first time, your screen will probably look like the one above.

When you already have those lessons, they should turn up on this home screen. Use the "+" button to add new classes.

Google may ask if you are registered with G-suite after clicking on the "+" sign.

Using Classroom at a school with students?

If so, your school must sign up for a free G Suite for Education account before you can use Classroom. Learn More

G Suite for Education lets schools decide which Google services their students can use, and provides additional privacy and security protections that are important in a school setting. Students cannot use Google Classroom at a school with personal accounts.

☐ I've read and understand the above notice, and I'm not using Classroom at a school with students

GO BACK   CONTINUE

Most than certainly you have a Google account, and the IT provider of the school district has enrolled for G Suite for Education. The organization must be licensed by a school official when the system has not yet enrolled, and the employees and the students must set up a Google account. That person will also need to make sure that the Google Classroom is switched on, and have you as a course-building mentor. Legally, the firm or school has/does make a G suite wallet.

The best thing about Google Classroom is that it is self-contained and only users in the jurisdiction can access it, and it provides a degree of protection for school-age children. On the other side, irrespective of the laws about privacy, you must remember that you cannot share your classroom with someone in the jurisdiction of the institution. Guardians can have summaries on their student success via email if the option is turned on.

3. Fill in your class information

You have to add your class tag. It is how the students recognize the class when Google Classroom opens.

Use the field "Section" to distinguish between different classes of the same type. For a class time, several teachers can use this area. (Optional to use in this field).

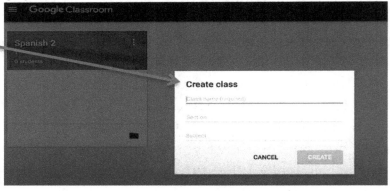

The "subject" field allows you to choose, or type your own, from a list of class subjects.

Having a new class contributes to the creation of current classwork, and students of the other three beneficial sections respectively. "TOPICS" is at the core of the "Classwork" page. This page allows the teacher to categorize assignments into groups.

Additional topics are applied at the end of the "classwork" page by example, and that involves shifting topics up, down as you require them. Many teachers seem to be very unsatisfied with this feature. Arrangements of different topics can also be done by those features of the "classwork" page.

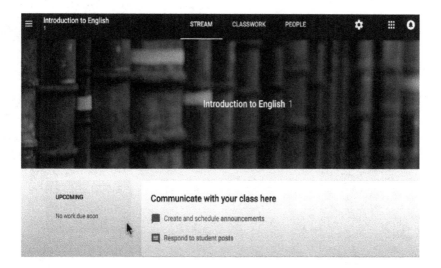

4. Students will start joining after your class is formed

Students can attach a join code to your class (above). This is a simple and fast way to bring students into your college. Students can log in to Google Classroom by displaying the join code, click the "+" button, and "Join Class" to enter the join code. They'll then be added to your class. You will send students to your study. It is a reasonable choice if the students do not meet for your class in person. Click on the "People" tab at the top to do this. Then press the button "Invite Students" (an individual symbol, and a plus). If all students are in a classroom group at Google, you can invite students individually with email addresses or by groups. The moment you build it there won't be any students in your study. This is the time for creativity and fun with it."

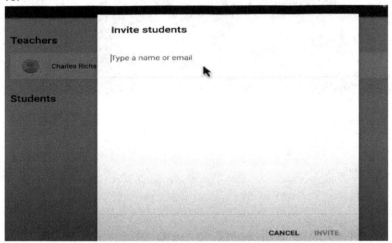

5. Select "Style" at the header's right side. It will open a gallery of photos with headers that you can use to jazz up your classroom

You can also upload a photo at the top of your classroom for viewing. You can use a picture of your class, or something related to your class. With important facts and pleasant graphics, some teachers can build a custom header picture.

4.1 To Create a Custom Header Using a Template

For page, like most Google apps, you will start engaging for your community, Google Classroom offers a "Feed" of sequential articles where tasks, queries, and other events are placed down. Scrolling was too laborious because of the previously added posts, according to educators. As a better suggestion was made, a new segment on classroom organizes material by classes, and groups, making it easy for educators to schedule their courses by course, and category, furthermore it enables students to locate assignments more easily. For activities that illustrate questions and communications further, also the stream is restored with a seamless vision. It makes this platform a stronger communication platform where teachers can tell their students about when to submit their work, press updates, etc. Students can even comment online offering a virtual platform for classroom.

Some features that were recently released include a better understanding and group that helps to better handle co-teachers, pupils, and guardians. Google's Classroom lets teachers connect, uninstall profiles, change guardian information. Resources are standardized. Teachers can change the description of the class, course code can also be edited, and the class location, and manage how students interact with each other, how they can post on the stream. Further changes by Google have also been released, which include is to padlock a Chromebooks screen while a quiz is running. After the screen has been locked students are not able to change screens or tabs, but this cheating restraining is only the feature of Chromebooks. So the stream page helps you to build unique messages, unique alerts, or replay previous clicks. This can be achieved in Google Classroom for all students in the school or limited courses. Thus, such posts produced by the maker may be for any audience or student, or a particular group of students. You may use documents, images, recordings, and files to support this article or comment. At the moment it was written, the students will see this report, or it can be scheduled for some date in the future too. The stream page lets the teacher respond to student messages. After a range of updates has been made, the very first post will be moved down the queue, and the new post will appear at the top of the list.

Join or start a meeting ✕

Enter the meeting code or nickname. To start your own meeting, enter a nickname or leave blank.

Learn how to schedule a meeting in Calendar   **Continue**

Chapter 5: Customize Your Google Classroom

Students will not be present in your class the moment you create it. Now is the creation time, and a little fun! Tap "Select theme" on the right side of the header. It will open an image gallery with headers that can be used to energize your classroom.

For sharing, you can also post a screenshot at the top of your Google Classroom. You might be using an illustration linked to your subject, or anything specific to your education. To create a custom header picture, some teachers can use essential details, and fun graphics. You may also use any template to build a custom header.

Pick a topic inside Google Classroom. There's still the chance to use Google Meet in Google Classroom. Google has added the capability Google Meet directly from your Google Classroom!

- How to build a Google Meet connection in Classroom

In your Google Classroom, click the "Settings"

icon. Scroll from there down to "General."

Click "Meet Link Generate."

Click on "Visible to Students" to see, and view this connection while logging in to Classroom.

Once the connection has been created, if you wish to distribute it, you can copy the link to another site. From here, you can only reset the link.

- How Google Meet can be used for e-learning, online learning

As students learn from home, it will be the one to use the connection you need with Google Meet.

- How to use Google Classroom in day-to-day class

Once the class is set up, you have a completely working Google Classroom, and the students have entered, but you don't wish to stop there. You are going to do certain things in your Classroom:

1. Create post and exchange updates with your class in Google Classroom.

2. Attach a note to:

This is a good way to communicate about your class and give them up-to-date information. Announcements are reported on the class stream but are not connected to a ranking. Go to your Stream account and press "share with your friend" Attach text to the post. Link other files (attached or from a Google Drive), YouTube links, or connections if you wish. Then post it (or plan it to later).

3. To make a request, to ask, to add material or to reuse an old message.

This is where the students can post their assignments to work! You can construct a graded (or ungraded) student response query, a quiz, or student answering tasks. This can be created under the "Classwork" tab (top). Also, incorporating material that you want to use or revisiting an old school story.

5.1 GOOGLE CLASSROOM ALLOCATION TIPS

I. Objects and items (above) to include in your task or question.

II. A concise title for your assignment: (Pro tip: it is great to number the assignments to avoid confusion).

III. A brief description: this is useful for the students who are missing, and for later returning to a previous task so that everyone can complete their work.

IV. Points: select the number of points worth the assignment/question (or use the option to un-grade the assignment).

V. A deadline: choose when the assignment is due (or pick no deadline date).

VI. A topic: (what the function in question is about).

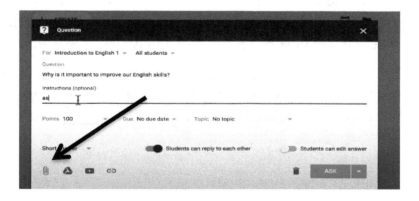

• Find attachment: attach data, attach Google Drive data, provide YouTube videos, or include a connection to the students.

Immediately delegate the task, plan it to publish automatically later, or save the task as a draft for later completion.

• Arrange subjects in your study.

If you have different chapters, units, topics, etc., in your class, you can categorize your assignments and topic-by-topic questions to keep all organized.

Under "Classwork," click the "Create" button, and add a link to it. Once you make a new assignment or statement, you will then be required to add the topic to it.

• Rating to, and job return.

When students have finished their studies, you may have feedback and task ranking. To view student research, tap the "Classwork" tab, and then tap the assignment.

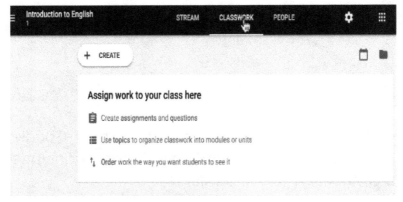

• Here are a couple of the things you will be learning:

I. Sort the assignment by the students who turned the job into the students who got the assignment or all that. (Simply click the big number) Or you can use the drop-down menu to filter other choices under the big numbers).

II. Click to open and view the work of the student. Within student papers, slide shows, etc., you can add remarks directly to the paper.

III. Tap the name of the student to write, and show the user's private remarks, and when the context files were hand in, you'll see.

IV. Add a degree of work with the school.

V. Once you're all done, return the work to the students. Check the box next to the initials, and click the button "return."

VI. On Google Classroom, tips, and techniques.

5.2 Tips for Improving Google Classroom Usage

Here are just a few tips for improving Google Classroom usage.

1. To reorder them on your "students" page, pick, and push your class cards across the screen (press the "three Lines" menu button, and the "set").

2. Whenever you see a folder, click for that section in Google Drive, push it to reach the Google Classroom window. This is where you see the students' work when it is delivered.

3. Assignments of due dates immediately transfer to the account on Google Calendar. Tap on the "Calendar" icon to display it.

4. Want to create an independent copy of every student's assignment file? (You have a multimedia organizer that ALL students should complete.) Google Classroom is like your automatic photocopier. To add the file to your request, use the drop-down menu on that file, and then select "Make a copy for each student."

5. The Google Classroom mobile app is your secret tool for providing students fast, easy,

immediate feedback. Check out what you can do in this respect.

6. Using the "gear" icon from your Google Classroom home screen, change your account settings. You can change the name of your class, display the class code, determine what actions students can take in the stream, and decide to display deleted items.

7. Organize by modules or by units

8. Organizing by study unit: teachers establish themes for each class to coordinate by study unit, and put under the subject all tasks for that specific unit. This approach had been Google's original purpose with the redesign.

5.3 HOW TO ORGANIZE GOOGLE CLASSROOM TASKS

I.   Organization by Week:

For each week, several teachers create a new theme, either by naming them "Week # 1," or by naming it "September 10-14 Week." It relies solely on the theme of the instructor for work and college.

II.   Form of Organization by Assignment:

Teachers arrange tasks by job category in this system, such as "Daily Work," "Projects," "Tests," etc. Remember that the company and the pupils alike are about you. Will students get to understand job forms? Remember to keep things up to the age level you're teaching user-friendly.

III.   Organize   by   Topic   Areas   (best elementary):

Organizing by topic field sounds more appropriate to primary teachers who teach several topics.

IV.   Organize Topic by Adding the Topic "Today":

This one is usually combined with one of the tips provided above. Lots of teachers are suggesting it. The idea is to create a special theme called "Today," where you manually move every item you want students to focus on that day. Then push the word "Today" to the top of the page because it's on the front and middle for your pupils.

V.   Organize by Targeted Learning:

The teacher assigns numbers, letters, and

objectives for learning, and uses them in the subject, and task. If you don't have a stand, uniform markers, this is a great solution to having students relate the project to the purpose of their assignments.

VI.   When to Program Electronic Missions

Hint: allow display warnings for assignments

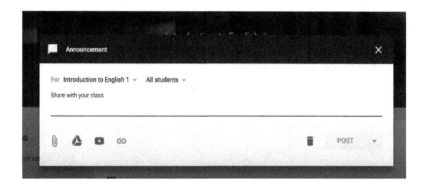

One thing that tends to drive certain teachers mad is that the assignments are still published in the "Sea." If this appears to you to be an inconvenient approach, this choice may be deactivated to prevent ambiguities.

To disable this feature, go to your class and press the "Setup" icon in the top right corner. Scroll down to "Normal."

Tap the "Classwork on the stream" drop-down button next to, and pick "Hide notifications."

Tip: Create a Past Assignment Thematic.

The phenomenon is that some instructors enjoy tossing out old tasks. Unfortunately, once they've finished, you can't make tasks disappear.

Build a topic called "Past assignments," or something that makes sense to explain to both you and your students. Drag the topic down to your "Classwork" tab. Once an assignment has been completed or you no longer accept work, move it to that topic.

Chapter 6: Tricks and Tips to Use in Classroom Google

To keep your Google Classroom light on eyes is to make sure to assign numbers. This lets you not only manage Classroom data better but also maintain Google Drive secure and consistent.

- To Find Numbers and Phrases in Classroom Easily

Few weeks of assignments later, although you may have a very organized Google Classroom, it is bound to become lengthy. Hence, to further organize it better and to check for specific words or numbered assignments (stated above) on the tab, you may do this by using the (Control + F) (Command+F on a computer). Teach that trick to student too!

- Organize Google Classroom by "Topics"

If you want to keep your Google Classroom tidy, then use the "topic" tab on the classroom page to help arrange student and instructor assignments. There are many other ways you can use to organize your Google Classroom. This can be done and teachers may find it easy than the rest of the tips available. For students, this is a real choice. Pick a technique that fits with your region and you and your students' style of content.

- Make it Easier for Students to Find Material (Commonly Used)

Every class has a specific assigned place to collect materials, connections, class guidelines, and syllabus, and so on. It has been recommended that you build a separate folder and class content subject and hold it near to the upper part of Google Classroom for easier access. Make sure to specifically assign specific code these files and students realize precisely what's in there.

- Create a Template for Google Classroom

When you have decided on your preferred way of organizing for your digital classroom (already checked it!), then make sure to duplicate it for your convenience. You can keep making a copy whenever you are about to teach a new class coming year and you will find it easier than before because all the contents have always been created and ready to use.

If you want to create a duplicate of a Google Classroom class then go to your Google Domain account, then press 3 dots and select the option

Chapter 6: Tricks and Tips to Use in Classroom Google

To keep your Google Classroom light on eyes is to make sure to assign numbers. This lets you not only manage Classroom data better but also maintain Google Drive secure and consistent.

- To Find Numbers and Phrases in Classroom Easily

Few weeks of assignments later, although you may have a very organized Google Classroom, it is bound to become lengthy. Hence, to further organize it better and to check for specific words or numbered assignments (stated above) on the tab, you may do this by using the (Control + F) (Command+F on a computer). Teach that trick to student too!

- Organize Google Classroom by "Topics"

If you want to keep your Google Classroom tidy, then use the "topic" tab on the classroom page to help arrange student and instructor assignments. There are many other ways you can use to organize your Google Classroom. This can be done and teachers may find it easy than the rest of the tips available. For students, this is a real choice. Pick a technique that fits with your region and you and your students' style of content.

- Make it Easier for Students to Find Material (Commonly Used)

Every class has a specific assigned place to collect materials, connections, class guidelines, and syllabus, and so on. It has been recommended that you build a separate folder and class content subject and hold it near to the upper part of Google Classroom for easier access. Make sure to specifically assign specific code these files and students realize precisely what's in there.

- Create a Template for Google Classroom

When you have decided on your preferred way of organizing for your digital classroom (already checked it!), then make sure to duplicate it for your convenience. You can keep making a copy whenever you are about to teach a new class coming year and you will find it easier than before because all the contents have always been created and ready to use.

If you want to create a duplicate of a Google Classroom class then go to your Google Domain account, then press 3 dots and select the option of "copy class."

- Using Clear Engagement References

You can also tell your students about a particular assignment. This step makes it easier for students to get back to a given activity so simple. For this, go to the "Classwork" page, find the assignment, right-click on the three dots, and duplicate the link.

- Google Classroom Has Space for Saving Syllabus

Most teachers utilize Google Documents also known as Docs to build a syllabus, such that it can be modified over the year as a live text. Include links to external material, videos, helpful content, and assignments.

- Divide Assignments Into Different Steps

Assignments that require project-based learning is very fundamental to student's mental and social growth, and you need to think uniquely about how you implement it in your classrooms as any one of the assignment is equally important.

For students, lengthy projects can be daunting, particularly those who haven't learned how to handle their time. Giving them achievements and splitting the work into smaller tasks with checkpoints, is critical. It is just the best solution, so the students will not feel pressured.

- Build a Special Class for Development

To complete your work before time in your class doesn't have to they are free to do as they please. This could include literacy and learning opportunities for pupils. You should make a different class within your Google Classroom for this purpose.

- Use Remote Comments for Feedback and Student Conversations

Some of Google Classroom's favorite app is its anonymous message interface. This little method will help streamline connectivity and boost the feedback loop with your students. Some critical variables of student development are the input from instructors!

Private remarks between teachers and students are just that—private. (Nobody can understand it).

Please note to use private feedback and keep an eye on your student's progress!

So this doesn't remove the influence of one-on-one meetings, in retrospect, it helps the students so they can recall the suggestions, these further give students and the ability to connect with those students who don't usually talk in the community.

Different places are available in Google Classroom to message privately

- At the Beginning of the Student Page, on Which They Work:

Tap on the task you want to offer reviews on from the classwork page.

Tap on "View Assignment," from the left side of the list select your student.

You can select "Add Private Comment" at the end of the right and row.

Tap to log in and submit your student's private message.

You may now also apply private remarks from within the student's paper using the latest rating function of Google Classroom.

- Use the Grading Tool to Privately Message:

Tap on the task in the "Classwork" tab on which you want to comment and give a grade.

Tap "View Assignment."

Tap on the student file you want to offer input on.

To make a private message, use the panel at the top.

- Private Feedback Functionality

Many instructors take private feedback functionality to solidify it as the portion of the task by asking students to provide thought by commenting privately on the statement after presenting their task. Using a discussion in which anyone in the class can comment was proposed, or offering students a suggestion like, how was the assignment? Which aspect of you is challenged? Avoid adding this instruction, so students won't forget!

For each assignment attach an "Outlining Document." This suggestion has been seen on many occasions too.

To each assignment attach an empty page of Google Document/template as a duplicate on behalf of every student. Teachers can see the assignment sheet in Google Classroom and provide a thumbnail for respective students. That lets you see development at a glance or lack of it. If you don't have a Google Doc for your work, it's suggested that you attach a blank document to be used as a template so you can still see the progress of your students.

Invite teachers who are reluctant, for them to co-instructor in your class to use Google Classroom. With Google Classroom, not every instructor is on track.

When you deal with an instructor who is reluctant or maybe even technophobic, encourage them to enter as a pupil or co-instructor in your class. Invite them at least as a beginner and they have an understanding of how it functions until they are granted the opportunity to incorporate and update the class as a co-teacher.

Within a college, co-teachers should do everything you want.

Inviting Teachers:

- Open the Page of the Respective Google Classroom

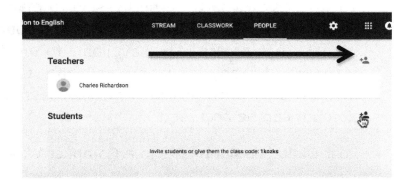

Click on the "People" tab that is on the top of the page.

To invite any teacher as a co-instructor, click the "invite teachers" icon. It can be done by providing specific emails and code.

- Create a Student Account for Demonstration Purposes.

    Currently, Google Classroom is not offering teachers a way to look into any classes as students and you will have a school account to access your class as a member. A solution, it has been mentioned, to use a sample account to sign in as a guest. So later on, you can demonstrate how the classroom side functions to see how the students will use the Classroom.

    Based on the school this may not be as easy to do.

    This is easy if you have permission to make Google Accounts in the domain of your school. That access is not available to most teachers. In any situation call the tech mentor or IT tech to see whether a trial account can be accessed.

- Post Digital Assignments in a Compact Way

To enhance how students require your specific instructions and what they require as instruction is in a compact, easy to access the folder.

The more details you include in the task, the fewer concerns you need to answer to and the less reasons students will have for failure to finish the project and on schedule.

Chapter 7: Google Classroom as Gamification?

Gamification is a strategy utilized by programmers to incorporate simulation features into non-gaming environments, such that customer interaction with a product or service will be improved. Through mixing in an established program suitably enjoyable elements, such as leaderboards and awards, programmers exploit the inherent desires of consumers so they love utilizing it more and also learn from it.

7.1 GOOGLE CLASSROOM AS GAMIFICATION

These ways can be used to gamify Google Classroom:

- **Socrative**: Socrative contains other community games, formational evaluations, and the immersive test game Space Sprint. Students are praised for tests for success, and instructors are encouraged to interpret outcomes. Socrative has a Chrome app and the option to sign-in with Google. Activities with the "Share to Classroom" extension for Google Chrome may be useful for pupils.

- **Class craft**: Class craft is an engaging management system that interfaces with Google Classroom. It transforms student success into a level playing game and bonuses that teachers may select or modify. The instructors will even transform current classes into customized experiences for the students themselves. Class craft helps teachers to incorporate PBIS with no additional work. The simple package is free and encourages parents to gamify classroom scheduling, customize characters and apps.

- **Book Widget**: Book Widgets offers teachers with over 40 free models to build immersive lessons for learners. There are models for playing, experiments or feedback, usability, and more. Integration into Google Classroom is easy with the Book Widgets plug-in for Chrome. Click the create button on the page, and then. To open the interface, press the "Book Widget" button. Select the widget you like and start creating.

- **Quizziz**: Quizziz helps teachers to take advantage of already made quizzes or build their own. Schools can also use live mode, and students can use homework mode independently of each computer. Students are also able to play one-on-one games with other users worldwide. Quizziz monitors pupil success and instructors can use the tests to recognize strategies and opportunities for remediation. Quizes can be exchanged by beginning a live or homework game with Classroom. There is a "Share to Classroom" button on the homework game code tab, and a "Share Via" button exists on the live game code list.

- **Kahoots**: to Google Classroom another popular game-based learning resource is Kahoots. Multiple-choice questions are created by teachers by using the platform, which transforms the students into a fun, interactive game. Students may respond to questions using any computer. Kahoots may be performed as a group in class, or teachers may give a Kahoots as a home-based task. Chrome has a Kahoots feature, so problems relevant to the platform can be communicated via Google Classroom.

- **FlipQuiz**: FlipQuiz is a competitive, quite similar to *jeopardy*. Teachers are required to sign in using Google authorizations to build student evaluation apps. You can share your games in Google Classroom using the Google Chrome "Sharing to Classroom" extension.

- **Prodigy Math**: Prodigy Math is free of cost math-based game, which can be tailored to match different requirements for students in grades K-8. It includes a diagnostic test, integrated tests, and differentiated instruction. Prodigy Math is united into Google Classroom, so there's even a Chrome version.

- **Breakout EDU**: the Breakout EDU lets teachers and students build and distribute content-aligned interactive games that can be incorporated into Google Classroom. Using an escape game technique, students utilize teamwork and logical reasoning to attain teacher-set objectives.

- **BrainPOP**: BrainPOP is an active teaching-learning site where students can take advantage of games and animation to help them understand the content better. All school and system users have the right of entry to connect with Google Classroom.

- **Bingo**: Bingo is the first game of playing! You can add your pictures or words from the Book Widgets directed to the Bingo widget, and share the results with your students.

Every student gets another sheet set of bingo.

I. Word bingo: write a term's meaning, and then let the student locate the word on the board.

II. Image bingo vocabulary: using cards with images of the words (translated) you call out.

III. Minimal pairs of bingo: using pairs of words differing in a single sound

IV. Rhyme Bingo: mark the terms on the bingo card in rhyme.

V. Decimal Bingo: place the decimals on the card and then simply read out the digits, or as fractions.

VI. Headshot bingo: place on the card pictures and/or descriptions of all the students in the class and potentially complete the list of faculty leaders, instructors, principal, address someone by name, or provide hints to the person you are talking to.

VII. Typing Scout: Typing Scout is free of charge forum for students to practice, by playing, keyboarding skills. The "Share to

Classroom" Extension will transfer material to Google Classroom.

- Crossword

The crossword puzzle is one of the most-used learning apps. You will do it the same way: you offer a description and you have to find the correct word for the students. A crossword puzzle can be more than that as you can see in the proof!

Use puzzles with crosswords with:

Science: it's not convenient to know the elements in the periodic table. If you place the symbols and their titles in a crossword puzzle, it certainly is a lot more interesting.

Geography: Geography always has a fair share of names to remember: nations, towns, oceans, mountain ranges, rivers.

Languages: adaptations will be made while you are teaching a foreign language. Let the students translate the provided word into the language you are teaching.

The crossword puzzle has a choice for automated scoring. Let the students apply their completed crossword puzzle in Google Classroom and take a peek!

- Jigsaw Puzzle

Upload an image, pick, and create how many parts you like. It is this easy! It's efficient to build a puzzle in Google Classroom using Book Widgets! A jigsaw puzzle is a lot of fun, so what is this game's learning value? Let your students solve geographic puzzles involving a region, a nation, a planet. This way, they realize where everything in the universe belongs.

Let the students solve a picture puzzle, depicting a specific setting or historical individual. They have to say what they learn about the location or person on the picture in geography class or history class. Let the students solve a picture mystery with a jigsaw. A photo of the bedroom for a starter. Students will turn whatever they see on the picture into a foreign language. They master the language this way. Playing a platform puzzle game in Google Classroom.

- Memory

A game of memory is used to train the memory of your students and can be used to form associations. Many things like multiple chickens, one hammer. When one student sees a similar set, the other student is asked what it is like. Students turn on the switch. When one student sees a similar pair, they tell the similarity to the other student. Students click on the light. The students can now make associations.

- Randomness

It is undoubtedly a game you haven't played before on. This game includes wheels with pictures, emoticons, numbers, and words, etc. Spin the pedals, and look what happens. Let the students make up their scenario about something provided randomly. What a perfect practice to talk or to compose!

Certain choices are to:

Let the students construct a correct phrase with words provided by the random widget. For instance: You-to talk-Great future. Run likelihood tests. Dice roll or flip coins. Get to know one another. Ask students to add headshots of themselves in one wheel, and a topic like "hobbies" they've got to talk about on each other. Add wheel numbers. Spin the drum, and let the numbers be multiplied, split, subtracted, or removed.

- Pair Matching

This game looks very much like "Memory." The main distinction is that students will fit pairs, without needing to recall their position. Taking this definition by look: Here is some other collaboration you may make:

- o Terms and translation
- o Photos and a description of them
- o Arithmetic and a fix
- o Photos showing people and their names
- o Monument images and their names/places
- o Terms and meanings

- Spot the Difference

A lot of learning styles are compared to each other in schooling. Knowing the differences is important for the students. Spot the difference in e-learning is exactly what you need. Here's some extra inspiration: you might bring two pictures of ancient building designs together and ask students to clarify the distinctions, so what about the distinctions between plants, species, ecosystems, countries, ancient civilizations, nations, soldiers, you name it!

- Hangman

This is such a renowned game. This is sometimes used as an energizer or as a buffer for classes. But that can also have an educational value.

Using the game Hangman: presenting you as a teacher. What are your favorite foods/hobbies? Let us guess the students. Presenting a new concept or subject. To help students pronounce rough terms correctly, to sum up, a topic or tale with just a few words. These terms are important keywords for students to speculate.

Can you imagine my favorite meal? Hangman coaching game at Google Classroom.

- Word Search

That is a tricky one. Many students will easily recognize phrases; some just don't. For most instances, only find the provided terms for the students. But still, you should spice up stuff.

Many scientific topics come to know a lot of jargon. Word quest puzzles are ideal for the job of immersive presentation of science vocabulary. Want geography? Names of continents, nations, towns, rivers, mountains, send a nation's capital and make students check in the word search for the right place. Students could look for the translation of the given word when they were teaching languages. Students may look up the written number for the little ones because they know how to write down an amount.

- Mind Map

Most of the time a mind map is used to focus on ideas or to remember, to learn information. One mind map can also be used:

o Creating a Definition

o To Sum Up a Theme/Theme

o Mapping Ideas

o To Ask Questions About a Subject

o Showing Yourself

Chapter 8: Apps and Sites That Work Well With Google Classroom

You may be familiar with apps and sites that integrated well with Google Classroom or you may be wondering what integration even means. That breakdown should help either way. Google Classroom essentially utilizes an API (application program interface) for communicating and exchanging knowledge with all of your favorite devices. Integrate hundreds of applications and websites, and we'll show a couple of our choices below.

Integrations with Ed-tech may seem overwhelming, but it has been boiled down to the basics. Below are three main approaches to streamline the operation of the classrooms:

1. Import Classroom rosters via an app or web platform.

2. Once a roster has been shared between an app and Classroom, manage the coursework and submissions that incorporate content from that app.

3. To share content from a website into the

Classroom, search the Google Share button.

If you have Google Classroom and some of the resources mentioned below, combining them would ease the teaching-cycle even further.

- Import class rosters

Teachers can import Google Classroom classes into websites, such as Pear Deck, BrainPOP, and Typing Club. The interface with Pear Deck helps teachers to upload a class roster, and then invite, and watch each student from their computer when they enter the Pear Deck class session. Integration of BrainPOP continues with the Google App, which teachers may navigate from the Google Apps Launcher app. Importing a Google class will build student accounts in BrainPOP; students can then sign in to get started in the program through the Google Launcher menu. Teachers can update their synced class roster by adding to or removing Classroom students. To lovers of Google Classroom, there's no question that this two-way syncing can save you time.

- Assign classes and plan requirements for students

If you have exchanged a class roster from Classroom and resources, such as Actively Learn, Tynker, or Classcraft, synchronizing instructor tasks, student presentations, and grades is that much simpler. For example, teachers can delegate a reading lesson to a class in Google Classroom directly from the Actively Learn site. The teachers will then publish the grades to the Classroom after evaluating an assignment to "Actively learn." Similarly, teachers may assign a coding lesson to a Classroom stream for students to access directly from the Tynker site. Within Tynker, students will then translate into a task, and teachers provide a review in their Classroom line.

Changing from Classroom and a subject-specific or instructor resource with ease—and then once again—helps teachers to utilize a range of applications and resources while ensuring that their student knowledge is being stored and modified.

8.1. SHARE SITE MATERIAL TO GOOGLE CLASSROOM

The Sharing in Google Classroom click allows it simple to distribute material directly in your Google Classroom from an app or website. Thousands of platforms that combine their material in this way like Newsela, Khan Academy, and CK-12. When teachers find something they want to share, it is easy to click the "Share" button, select a class, and then share the content with the students as an assignment or announcement. Typically the "Share" button is grouped among the usual selection of social media icons; the same types of content that you have been able to share on Twitter or Facebook can now be shared in the same way in Classroom.

1. CK-12

You won't believe the insane number of free tools on CK-12. Assigning any of those items in Google Classroom is a breeze, and completion and grades are recorded in your Gradebook online.

2. Curiosity.com

Discover fascinating quick reads about just about every subject you might think, and then press a button to add them to your Google Classroom. Generally, these posts are best for middle and high school. Notice that this is an ad-supported platform.

3. DOGONews

The kid-friendly news articles on DOGONews

make it easy to assign reading to the discussions at current events. Each article is labeled with recommendations for the reading/interest stage and provides suggestions for use in common core and regional curriculum requirements for lesson plans. Assigning papers for reading is free; paid plans also include topics for debate and quizzes.

4. Ed Puzzle

Transform every video into an immersive tutorial online, or even upload your own. Add questions, audio, or notes that will allow students to watch and learn at their own pace. The tracking features allow you to monitor their progress and understanding, and to easily integrate with Google Classroom. The comprehensive, affordable package provides up to 20.s spaces at a time.

5. Explain Everything

Explain Everything is a whiteboard app and you can use it in the classroom just like you would an interactive whiteboard. Even better, it allows you to record your interactions and share them for students to view later via Google Classroom. The free version does have some limitations but offers a lot of cool features.

6. Flipgrid

Students record short posts with Flipgrid to react to topics that you delegate to them. This is a particularly cool app for students who hesitate to speak live on Zoom calls; it allows everyone to be heard. For Google Classroom it's easy to upload your grids and assignments.

7. GeoGebra

The GeoGebra devices do not look sophisticated, but they do have the flexibility for the students to keep Math concepts alive. This site has hundreds of resources that Math's teachers will love, including an online graphing calculator, from basic arithmetic to high-level calculus. It's a breeze for learners to exchange lectures, tests, quizzes, and more.

8. Google Cast for Education

This simple Chrome extension allows sharing the computer with someone a little breeze. Students share their screen with the teacher in a classroom setting (in-person or virtual), and the teacher shares it with the class using a projector or via Google Classroom. To any consumer, it is easy, free, and a must.

9. Khan Academy

Most teachers now realize the extremely wide variety of free online learning opportunities that

Khan Academy has to bring. We explore any stage of topic and degree and offer students the additional time we need to learn key concepts. Using your Google Classroom rosters, build and merge classes and all of you are ready to delegate materials.

10. Listen Wise

Every day, Listen Wise publishes a new episode with free current affairs you can share with your friends. Such brief audio lessons are perfect for the morning meetings or the launch of a general discussion of current affairs. Listen Wise Premium provides a broad podcast archive of tutorials, quizzes, and immersive annotations, which are now free for 90 days to download.

11. Math Games

Teachers of basic mathematics... this one is for you! Follow up your math lessons with these games of fun and free practice. Assign them as an alternative to dull old worksheets for school, or children needing additional practice.

12. Nearpod

Nearpod is an easy-to-use tool for collaboration, with so many educational applications. Teachers launch aboard and post a query or response, then submit their responses or opinions to the students. Even you can post videos. Nearpod is a great way to incorporate reminders for learning, study for an exam, obtain tickets for the virtual exit, and many more, and it fits beautifully with Google Classroom. The free version has a decent amount of storage and all the basic features.

13. PBS Learning Resources

PBS has a vast array of resources on every imaginable topic, all easy to share in your virtual classroom. Each pattern matched. Includes recommended grade ranges and instructional tools to help you and the students make the best of it.

14. Quizizz

Quizizz is a fun resource to help students analyze what they know in the classroom. Choose one of the thousands of already accessible quizzes, or build your own. Host live online quiz games in class or use Google Classroom to allocate them as homework. Customize each task to show how many times each query should be tried by a subject and how they have the right responses until they are done—instant input that allows studying more interesting.

15. Quizlet

This is one of the most common flashcard apps online, and it's safe. Throughout their vast collection, locate the flashcards you like or make your own to help some sort of tutorial. Share the flashcards with Google Classroom to provide students with easy exposure to these interactive resources at school or home.

16. Science Buddies

This link is the best buddy to any science instructor. It's filled with free posts, lesson plans, and tests, all searchable by grade and topic matter. This is also a fantastic go-to during the science fair season, with a galore of scientific method materials, science fair preparation methods, and a massive archive of project ideas. When using Science Buddies with Google Classroom, you'll also get access to additional quizzes and evaluations.

17. Wakelet

You should think about Wakelet as a collaboration method to get knowledge coordinated and exchanged. Using it to build and exchange lessons with your students by gathering media of your feedback and examples all in one place. Much better, students get it included in Google Classroom to build lectures, book reviews, newsletters, and more correct.

18. Workbench

Workbench is a set of teachable lessons and clicks on all sorts of topics. Find and delegate current classes, or build a personalized class on your own. Embedded posts, provide instructions, and even set up complete projects for students to complete the resources on this website.

Chapter 9: Advantages of Allowing Good Use of Google Classroom

Accident Report Forms – Build accident report forms for instructors and coaches in a Faculty Classroom to disclose injuries immediately to the office.

Book Reviews – Help students build book reviews to communicate with classmates, and the instructor uses Google Docs or Slides.

Booster Clubs – Use space for booster clubs in schools. Organizers will publish school activities, updates, and fundraising details to keep participants updated.

Flyers - Create flyers using tablets, computers, and images in Google Docs.

Make adventure in the classroom a reality by using Google Classrooms' posts Forms, Docs, Slides to build your own activity experiences.

Classroom Newsletters – Build newsletters at the class level with Google Documents (Docs), can be saved as a File, and submit to Classroom; teachers can also ask students to create newsletters created as a part of a work assignment.

Google Classroom Awards – Make sure to keep an eye on incentives for students by Sheets or Files. In the Classroom, you can post the winners.

Use Color as a Means of Activity – Use Google Sheets to create a colored number of events for students.

Color Directories – Keep structured in Microsoft Drive – by different colored Classroom directories. The folder can be open up color shift choices after clicking on them.

Comic Strips – Let students use Google Slides to generate comic strips.

Connect at One Time with Google Class or Several Classes – Classroom may be used to connect with one or more classes at a time by picking participants from the "With" drop-down column.

Talk to Experts – Because Classroom takes no limits, interacting with experts can happen in any area of the classroom. Invite specialists to collaborate with the school or tasks.

Resource Area Inventories – Through

logging their reflections on different subject areas and submitting these to Classroom projects, students may build topic inventories.

Competitions – With the help of Google Classroom, it is easy to run competitions online and with your class or company.

Monitor How Students Communicate With an Add-on – Instructors will pick on how students can comment, the post they have attached. Students are provided with choices to change access or show data. Students are also provided a choice to receive different duplicates of the add-ons if cooperation is not necessary.

Transform PDFs, and Photographs to Text – Google Docs will transform PDFs and photos to text utilizing OCR technology. To do the conversion, you will have to open a Google document in Google Documents (Docs).

Transform Files to Google Documents to Edit – Select options like Upload Files to Google Document in Editor format in Google's drive locales to instantly convert any files of Word document, Excel sheet, and PowerPoint presentation to a Google Document when upload.

Make Group Rules – Members of Classroom directly can come through to collaboration to change and redefine group rules and regulations.

Show Student Research – View student research while staying invisible to students.

Dissertations and Thesis – Build a lab for students who want to complete their thesis and dissertations. Not only does it offer a way of communication between instructor and client, but it also offers a platform for pupils to raise questions and help each other.

Promote Problem/Solution-Based Thinking – Students pose questions to define and address a topic they are reading from an image-based book and novel while still interacting with the characters intricate in the situation. The artifact should be uploaded via Google Slides, Google Documents, or photo to the Classroom.

Task Schedule – Build a job timetable with Google Documents or Papers, and distribute via Classroom with teachers.

Interactive Visualizations – Google Sheets can be used to construct dynamically updated interactive maps and graphs.

Epub Books – Ask students to use Google Documents or Slides to create eBooks. It can be logging their reflections on different subject areas and submitting these to Classroom projects, students may build topic inventories.

Competitions – With the help of Google Classroom, it is easy to run competitions online and with your class or company.

Monitor How Students Communicate With an Add-on – Instructors will pick on how students can comment, the post they have attached. Students are provided with choices to change access or show data. Students are also provided a choice to receive different duplicates of the add-ons if cooperation is not necessary.

Transform PDFs, and Photographs to Text – Google Docs will transform PDFs and photos to text utilizing OCR technology. To do the conversion, you will have to open a Google document in Google Documents (Docs).

Transform Files to Google Documents to Edit – Select options like Upload Files to Google Document in Editor format in Google's drive locales to instantly convert any files of Word document, Excel sheet, and PowerPoint presentation to a Google Document when upload.

Make Group Rules – Members of Classroom directly can come through to collaboration to change and redefine group rules and regulations.

Show Student Research – View student research while staying invisible to students.

Dissertations and Thesis – Build a lab for students who want to complete their thesis and dissertations. Not only does it offer a way of communication between instructor and client, but it also offers a platform for pupils to raise questions and help each other.

Promote Problem/Solution-Based Thinking – Students pose questions to define and address a topic they are reading from an image-based book and novel while still interacting with the characters intricate in the situation. The artifact should be uploaded via Google Slides, Google Documents, or photo to the Classroom.

Task Schedule – Build a job timetable with Google Documents or Papers, and distribute via Classroom with teachers.

Interactive Visualizations – Google Sheets can be used to construct dynamically updated interactive maps and graphs.

Epub Books – Ask students to use Google Documents or Slides to create eBooks. It can be done by using third party printing software.

Handbooks – For emergency procedures build and share handbooks for emergency procedures using Google Document and Google Classroom.

Warning Forms for Employees – Create an employee notice form through Classroom. This form can be shared privately with employees.

ePub File – Download and ePub files utilizing the Google Docs "open as" function. You can read the ePub files on your tabs or smartphones.

Rooms to Be Escaped – Build Classroom wireless escape rooms. Virtual escape rooms have several tools on the internet.

Explore App – Using the Explore app to display relevant material and photos from your paper or the internet in some Google Documents, Sheets, and Slides.

SIS export – Some SIS applications will let you build automatically with the Classrooms of Google and turn on the auto-sync for the class for student information.

Online Courses Exploration – Classroom of Google is a perfect opportunity for students to introduce themselves to a learning experience that is online before they reach the physical classroom.

Extension Classes – Post-extension classes for those candidates who are way ahead of other students and have already learned the curriculum or early graduates.

Field Trip in the Form of a Report – Have children take their mobile phones to reach field trip work schedule, planning to meet points or field trip documentation.

Edit Mail – Use Gmail to prevent a bogged down inbox. Establish filters to prioritize what is needed most in the Google Classroom.

Person to Person Interactions – Make students taking on the personalities of individuals personally participating in a study case or age they make selected, then build a monolog that can be captured as video or files of audio then posted to Classroom.

Quick quiz – Google Sheets can be used to build interactive flashcards, combined with 3rd party software.

Food Records – Build and/or full food records for wellness programs in the Classroom.

Footnotes – As a fragment of a thesis paper let

students apply footnotes to a Google File.

Formative Tests – Build formative tests to validate the students' understanding. Self-grading formative tests may be created by presenting a new query in Google Classroom with the multiple-choice substitute, with survey questionnaire, or with third-party applications that communicate with Classroom;

Fundraiser Collection Notes – Using Excel Sheets to build collection reports for fundraisers that can be exchanged with all teachers who manage groups or sports.

Acquire Volunteers – By using Google Classroom for schools' activities, volunteer-based community activities.

Generic Response Sheets – Build standardized answer sheets for learners in Google Docs and can be sent straight to the tutor in the classroom.

Geocaching – Students will complete geocaching instructions from Classroom with mobile devices. You should only upload the guidance you need, and students will have fun performing things outside the classroom.

International Pen Pals – Let students get in touch with another nation or world use Gmail to communicate with students on the other side of the world.

Google Chrome – Classroom makes usage of Google's Chrome software much more effective. For hundreds of attachments and plugins included in the Google Chrome Website, Classroom choices are nearly unlimited.

Less Paper is Used – Bring it all into Google Classroom and you will require less paper.

Classes of Different Grade – Build grade-level classes to interact with instructors, or to work for all pupils in a school. At the high school stage, imagine getting a Google Classroom for increasing grade stage that may be used for specific grade details such as buying senior hats, senior bands, pictures of classrooms, etc.

Guardian descriptions – Allow the guardians to include summaries about what occurs every day, weekly, or annually in the community.

Visiting Faculty – Invite classroom staff. Use apps from third parties to feed the lecture digitally, or use videos for scripted lectures.

Lists – Build support lists for anything, mainly students that need extra guidance on a topic. Pupils may register to the database by Google Classroom's Excel Spreadsheet, Documents, or

Forms.

Reporting – By creating Google's Form that managers can use to notify supervisors on incidents.

Puzzles - Using the jigsaw puzzle method to allocate students to Classroom to read multiple parts of a document or essay.

Journaling – Let your students keep an online blog for personal reflection, fiction, nonfiction, or any topic that interests them.

Offer up to Date Classes – Using Google Classroom will help courses to be changed on the move. Simply sign in, and access the lessons to keep your students informed.

Focused group studies – Using Google Classroom will help the students stay focused and organized without a paper-based assignment.

Keyboard Command – You can use the keyboard's command and push through the scoring method more easily. People will use the space bar, tab button to travel from the keyboard through student research, with no need to take your handoff.

Live Financial Services Information – Using

finance features from Google to deliver results from live finance.

Leave Request Applications – Provide students to leave them as a school setting and applications to apply if they want to go out of school.

Live Vocabulary – Let students have vocabulary pictures on a frame. The picture offers students the ability to build a deeper link to the term.

Lyric descriptions – Let students chat about what they consider is the most beneficial piece of knowledge they have been taught in limited classes. That group can use their queue to compose a review and is the brand new lyrics for a song selected by the community.

Making Sure That All Students Take Interest in Questions – The function of the Classroom question makes it easier to guarantee that all students are interested in questions. Only take a glance at this topic to see how other students have responded.

Make-Up Job – Make-up function may be viewed by students missing from the classroom.

Research Paper for Media – Students may embed any form of media into an exploration study on Google Documents that include images or videos.

Meeting Points – Register, and after minutes of meetings at the Classroom with increasing service.

Participation Data Forms – Creating and publishing knowledge sources of party membership.

Collection of Tutor Text Links – Provide links in the form of text for Google Classroom students through uploading the connections as content.

Menus – Build student favor menus, or use Microsoft Word or Slides as a web-based project.

Work-post layout functions, with instances of students to use.

Modules – Construct units or lessons by the unit in the Classroom using the subjects feature.

Class Name Conventions – Develop a class naming scheme such that you can quickly find classes that you are teaching.

These are just a few of the best advantages of using the right way Google Classroom.

Chapter 10: How to Engage Students

Students come to class with their heads buzzing about missed quizzes, increasing pressure on homework tasks, and worries regarding the relationships of their peers. You might continue your class with a consistent schedule to help remove such distractions from your mind.

10.1 Start Classroom at Google with Welcome Notice

Students come to class with their heads buzzing about missed quizzes, increasing pressure on homework tasks, and worries regarding the relationships of their peers. You might continue your class with a consistent schedule to help remove such distractions from your mind.

Students can exchange "news breaking" or "what's up with you?" In teams, small groups, or in the entire school. An embracing practice helps students to unleash their most pressing thoughts and build new encounters room for them. It often builds student partnerships, as they share a little with their peers. Welcoming practices promote a feeling of identity as the classroom is an environment where students are welcomed not only for who they are, but where they are at a given moment.

This quick interaction should be converted directly into an opening activity that leads to day-learning. Together they will consider an interesting question, share responses to a brief quotation or sentence, or take time to focus on the previous day's studying. Instead of a passive action, an opening class with an emphasis on student involvement puts student speech at the forefront of the learning experience.

• Prepare a Fair Playing Area for Student Speech

Prioritize constructive participation and voice of students during the planning process, by asking:

How do students work together to solve issues, create higher-order ideas, lead to the development of a product, or otherwise consciously interact with the meaning of a lesson?

How much is the skill granted to students to talk at the front of the class, to write on the paper, or to demonstrate on the video document?

How are students communicating to an audience outside the classroom?

Will students have options about what job they are doing?

If the students are told to link what they are learning outside the school to their lives?

Hopefully, the courses will be places where students gain not only skills but also know who they are and who they want to be. The only way students can arrive at such realizations is by an individual as well as collective explorations to bring their perspectives to the conversation. Prioritizing student expression promotes a feeling of identity because learning environments are co-created between students and instructors.

• Tell Students Lives Outside the School

The students will be told that they appreciate who they are and understand the complexities of their existence. Many students would be visible instantly, and others will vanish into the background if we enable them—so we need to constantly interact with all students. These times of student listening and talking improve relationship-building and belonging.

They can do this by greeting students when they enter the classroom, small-class conferences, and instructor conferences. Throughout their study halls or lunch hours, we can plan "lunch and learn" sessions or invite students to help us perform student work or even add to the classroom logistics.

When students realize we appreciate what they have to tell, they would be more inclined to express their views and observations. It might sound like we have little time to interact with a student, but we have little time to do so. As John Hattie informs us, "One pillar for learning is a positive, caring, welcoming atmosphere in the classroom." Successful teacher-student relationships represent the trust students have in sharing their experiences.

• Questionnaire on Reviews

Asking for comments is another powerful way to improve student dialogue. We're never going to know what it truly feels like to be a student in our classrooms, only as much as we like to be because our teachers have all the responses we seek. During the year, we will receive feedback from them and implement (when feasible) their suggestions. Not only does student feedback guide instruction, but it also conveys that we value their viewpoint and that their perspectives are at the heart of the work that we do.

Hearing and honoring our pupils, we must show them that their thoughts will be valuable learning instruments for themselves and others—and change drivers in their classes and beyond.

• The Positive Approaches of Digital Education

Although interactive education needs many of the same skills needed to effectively teach in a brick and mortar classroom—critical ability, teamwork, communication, creativity, and, of course, learning and student enthusiasm—some strategies are especially useful when attempting to reach people who you will never face to face with.

Communicate regularly with the teachers. Via an interactive message hub, community group, or even input on teacher-scored events, this daily contact and coordination may occur in person or online. Offer incentives for the students to collaborate with peers. When the participant knows that the content needs to be understood, clarified, and/or checked-in a collective discussion or group activity, the temptation to "break the law" will be reduced.

Set the simplest expectations. While connectivity is one of the greatest advantages that immersive learning platforms can provide, continuous commitment, tempo, and progress objectives remain a critical component for sustaining student achievement.

Work for the students to achieve goals. To be on the same page on a realistic wage and improvement plan is important for teachers and students. This gives each student power over their individualized learning plan and duty to stay dedicated to their established goals.

• Using the Data-Driven Interactive Program for Individualized Learning.

Online education offers personalized material at its finest and reaches every pupil at their learning pace. This frees the capacity of the instructor to determine student progress and performance in evaluating awareness and understanding. In monitoring and reviewing student data regularly, teachers will better guide student learning and give support to the struggling students.

• Support a Shared Working Climate.

Evidence shows that immersive learning methods, in comparison to traditional hierarchical teaching strategies, enhance learning in which teachers and students respond to the content and flow of instruction together.

This two-way dedication fosters student-based learning and motivates higher academic achievements.

Chapter 11: Google Classroom (For Students' Ease)

As a student, the first thing you should do is to get the app, which can be downloaded in the app store for iOS or Android, titled simply Google Classroom, and you can connect to a phone, Mac, and Chromebooks via a browser tab by going to Google, signing in, and having the Classroom software on the right.

11.1 WHY CAN I ALLOW STUDENT USE OF GOOGLE CLASSROOM?

Once in, click on the "+" icon, and enter your teacher's class code, or this move is as easy as choosing the "Enter" alternative if you enter from an already-sent invite.

When enabled, a "stream" tab shows updates and provides places to add comments. It is a class statement, so the entire class will see it in the post as well. A tab on the left indicates significant days coming up, including the due dates for classification.

At the top is a tab entitled "Classwork," showing any assignments and questions that require attention. Select the query and you will address it explicitly, sometimes with multiple-choices, so a click to pick is all you need. Comments may be inserted here one more time. Choose "Private Message" on the right to speak directly to the instructor— perfect if you are suffering and in search of support, and don't want to inquire in a public manner.

11.2 HOW TO COMPLETE GOOGLE CLASSROOM ASSIGNMENT

Head into Google Classroom and pick the top portion of the "Classwork" tab where assignments are listed. Choose the correct one and carry out what directions are included. If you have a template to fill up a task, pick it and you'll be guided to the Google app that lets you edit.

For instance, a document in Google Slides may allow you to attach photographs and text. The teacher should set this out clearly, so it is easy to complete.

When completed, click "Send," and tell the

instructor that the job is done and ready to be signed. When you choose to jump back into the job to delete it, you may always pick "Unsubmit."

If your Classwork does not have a guide to work from, instead you should build one. To the right is a plus icon to pick the item you want to create. For starters, pick Google Docs to generate a new document that lets you into your job. When completed, there is a "Turn in" button at the top right to get it explained to the instructor.

If the task asks for a photo, or file, click the plus button, choose the picture or file, and choose "Upload," and from the right side menu click "Turn in," and the instructor gets the task.

11.3 WHAT TO LEARN IN GOOGLE CLASSROOM

The key reference point for class communications is the segment named "Stream." It will include researches for all to use and vote on.

If the teacher allows, there may also be the option of creating a new post that could become a thread in which others can comment. For starters, you might ask the rest of the class if someone else is frustrated with a tutorial, whether they know what's coming up, or whether there's someone else that might help with a tech issue.

There's the "people" tab on top for a more private mode of contact. That allows students to contact their teacher or teacher directly. Select the mail icon and it will open Gmail, where you can send a message directly.

I. Exit Tickets: the teacher may ask you to answer a question before students leave a class.

II. Wait Time: Google Classroom tells the instructor how many students answering the query are finished and how many are still to respond.

III. Share a Resource: students may share resources, such as videos and so on to validate their responses.

IV. Multiple Choices and Polls: the query style with multiple choices helps you to survey the community. It is useful if you want to learn, for example, which resources the students are using for a particular assignment or the subject they are involved in focusing on next.

- Ask Students to Ask a Question

  Invite students to ask a question. Teachers, for instance, can ask a question like–What questions do you have about this topic? This builds a dialogue community, which fosters peer learning.

  These are one of the few suggestions on how you can engage students in Google Classroom and how these suggestions may help you in creating a learning, beneficial environment for you and your students.

Chapter 12: Advantages of Using Google Classroom

1. Exploration of an Online Learning Site

A lot of colleges today require students to take at least one online class during their degree work. In reality, if you have a Master's degree in education, some of your online coursework may be eligible. Unfortunately, many of the students never had any online education experience. That's why, at a young age, you want to make sure that your students get as much exposure as possible. Google Classroom is a simple way for students to assist with this process as its super user-friendly, making it a perfect technology intro.

2. Easy Material Access

Google Classroom allows students exposure to good content, no matter where they are, since everything is shared online. The missing days with the rubrics or worksheets are finished. If required, missing students can conveniently access learning resources from home–this will also help save you and your students a lot of trouble in the long run.

3. Differentiation

Google Classroom is a great tool for differentiation because you can set up many different classrooms. When you focus on a subject in the classroom and have students that operate in two separate stages, actually build two new classrooms within the project. In this way, you can better reach out to those who struggle with their kind of work without making them feel bad or dumb.

It can help you execute homework on a more personalized level, and also reach out to certain pupils. You can even divide everyone into groups you think they can work the best in. Google Classroom is a smart, modular way to ensure sure every student receives what they need, and that you can quickly uninstall and reconstruct classes as you see them.

The teachers can easily distinguish guidance for learners via Classroom. Assigning lessons to the whole college, specific students, or student classes only requires a few basic steps while making tasks on the Classwork website.

4. Paperless

Google Classroom can virtually rid itself of paper

consumption when used to run a whole class. Both classwork can be done electronically as long as the students have connections to the internet. That means no copies for your district and essentially less revenue.

5. No Work Is Lost

Students cannot miss their job unless they have it directly in their hands. Since they normally work on Google Drive, all save instantly and arguments are diminishing. Students will achieve more organizational performance with a few brief tutorials about how to best utilize such online resources.

6. Commitment

It has been proven time and time again that the platform engages students. Google Classroom can help students get involved in the learning process, and stay engaged. For example, if you have students answering questions in the Classroom, other students may focus on those responses and expand learning about all students.

Overall it's definitely worth using Google Classroom. This will save you time and money, which can help you train your students much better for the future. Google Classroom's built-in applications allow getting to meet students and their parents a breeze. Teachers and students will submit emails, post into the web, submit private comments on tasks, and receive input on jobs. Teachers have complete control of comments and posts from the students. They can also communicate with parents through individual emails or through email summaries from Classroom that include class announcements and dates.

7. Easy Access

Google Classroom can be accessed through Google Chrome from any machine, or any mobile device, irrespective of platform. Both files shared by teachers and students are placed on Google Drive in a "Classroom" tab. Users will enter the Classroom wherever, anywhere.

8. Exposure

The classroom provides access to an online learning environment for pupils. Today, many university and college programs allow students to participate in at least one online class. Google Classroom access may help students transition beyond other learning management programs that are common in higher education.

9. No Wastage of Paper

Teachers and students won't have to shuffle

unnecessary amounts of paper because Classroom is paperless. When teachers upload assignments and assessments to the Classroom, they're saved to Drive simultaneously. Students may complete tasks and assessments directly from Classroom and even transfer their research to Drive. Students can access missed work due to absences and locate other resources that might be needed.

10. Save Time

The Classroom is a perfect time-saver. With all money being stored in one location and being able to reach Classroom everywhere, teachers would have more free time to perform certain activities. As Classroom is accessible from a mobile device, teachers and students can participate through their phones or tablets.

Both services for a college are commonplace with students. No need to buy a journal, take your pad, travel to a lecture room, or print an essay. You can instead view the lesson online, answer questions, and even submit work all at one location. This way, everything stays clean and ordered, and time is not spent in pursuit of missing resources for classroom usage.

11. Collaboration

The Classroom gives the students many

opportunities to work together. Teachers may encourage online conversations inside the Classroom between students and build community projects. Additionally, students can collaborate on teacher shared Google Docs.

Many digital natives are familiar with technology and would be more likely to utilize technology to assume control of their learning. The Classroom provides several opportunities to render learning social and immersive. This allows teachers to separate tasks, to incorporate images and web sites into classes, and to build community tasks for teamwork.

12. Feedback Forum

Providing students with positive input is a vital feature of all instruction. Inside the Classroom's grading tool, teachers can send feedback on assignments to each student. There's also the ability to create a comment bank for future use within the grading tool. Furthermore, the mobile app Classroom allows users to annotate work.

13. Analyzing Data

To make learning effective, instructors will evaluate results from tests and ensure students recognize learning expectations. Data from evaluations can be easily exported for sorting and analyzing into Sheets.

An easy way to use Google Classroom is by analyzing data. Google Classroom is extremely easy as compared to other LMS (Learning Management Systems) that have been common over the past decade. This doesn't require much time or experience to set up a new classroom. Our tech team practiced for around an hour, and at the end of the week, we had both set-up and managed a lab.

Google Classroom is designed to help you interact more effectively. You enter the students' email addresses just once, so contact is achieved in the platform. The instructor just has an email list, a chat list, and a Google Calendar immediately generated by joining the student in the classroom, and adding and removing students from class as needed is simple.

Google Classroom is designed to enable you to interact more efficiently. The communication tools are probably more critical than being simple to use and usable, but they are also quite powerful. As it's all Cloud-based, students no longer "lose" tasks. The correspondence is smooth while a student is out. Google Classroom just last month added a parent notification feature to keep parents informed about what's going on in the "classroom."

Google Classroom is more cost-efficient and environmentally friendly. Many teachers may not be sold on completely paperless schooling, particularly for younger learners. When it comes to copying and printing, it can be seen as a real advantage for schools to be more cost-effective. Because every student also has a laptop that links to the Web, every sheet of paper we save can just make the school more productive and environmentally friendly.

That's how students can get to know in the future... which is why you may let go of your hang-up "paperless." University campuses no longer require their five-page papers to be posted for undergraduates. As K-12 educators, we will take care of this and train our students for the future in which they will work. (Terminology used for officially funded school groups from kindergarten through grade 12 in other countries) colleges and institutions of higher education that meet the guidelines below.

14. Institutions With Verified Non-Profit Status

The government recognized fully certified non-profit organizations providing certifications that are nationally or globally accepted at the principal, secondary and third levels.

Homeschools are also licensed because the local homeschool agency tests them.

For students who struggle, it's better as long as you help them manage the device. (The device itself can sometimes be distracting, so it's necessary to manage that.) The explanation Google Classroom is great is that it offers them the operational edge.

Tasks never get lost and the teacher is already organizing every classroom, but navigating this has to be taught for these students. While students are digital natives, this does not mean they understand how adults are organizing their world to help them learn.

Collaboration outside of school (i.e., Flipped Classroom) becomes simpler with Google Classroom. Once again, it is cloud-based and available with a link from anywhere. Students are allowed to share assignments and work together from home to complete them. Collaboration isn't just about working with other peers in a group. Through posting a picture, an instructor will change the classroom to go live in the evening, allowing students to watch it that night and practice for a question about it the next day. The choices are infinite.

Planning for teachers is simple, and it is worth

the up-front effort. In Google Classroom more new features allow teachers to schedule future assignments. Designated assignments might be scheduled to go live in October on a Monday, and then close that Friday. If an instructor has an extended absence, she will be able to arrange the tasks and not have to rely on a sub to handle anything. Classrooms are also available from semester to semester and from year to year. Copying and pasting a lesson for the next generation of students might be awful for an instructor, so it saves some energy to have some items already in order (class syllabus, ranking standards, etc.).

Feedback is swift and functional by embedding the elements. One of the teachers can be helping the students perform a multiple-choice question while viewing the film. This improves interaction and responsibility, which helps the instructor to show outcomes at the end of the lesson, too. When students fail to reply with the right responses, she will instead cover the subject again.

If something needs to be added or fixed, Google listens and responds (from this came both the timing of the assignment and the parent communication). That also means teachers will need to continue learning as they use it.

15. Integrate It With Other Apps in Google

Google Classroom is easily compatible with Google Docs, Sheets and Slides. Offering a portal that syncs with other online platforms for schools on a limited budget offers a means for schools and students to get through the 20th century without wasting a lot on costly classroom apps.

Teachers can post assignments for students; they view them as tasks. When all the assignments are done, it is checked off by the student. A formal collection of job completion measures keeps us focused and tends to prevent uncertainty over the activities that are assigned to them.

16. Allowing Students to Communicate With Others

Google Classroom has one function of generating tasks, such as queries. You should set up how many points a topic is worth, and also have students communicate. A forum that is easy to access, even in an online environment, facilitates interaction and allows students to learn from each other.

Besides the students collaborating, the teacher can contact via email with each student separately and with their guardian/parents also posts to the "stream" page. Even you may create a class notice that extends to all enrolled students.

17. Virtual Classroom Portal

Most universities now use a combination of classroom environments online and in real life. Using Google Classroom offers you exposure with either an instructor or a pupil in an online world.

You can even sign up as a student if you're an instructor and check how the program functions if you can direct some frustrated students a little. As the environment is more liked, including for topics like digital marketing, where students can now access a pre-recorded online class and upload research with a whiteboard or files attached, anticipate even further online classes.

18. Provide Tutorials in Audio

YouTube is an easy site to use, and Google Classroom enables you to either incorporate a video produced on a subject by someone else, or build your video, and upload the embed code via URL. The video lessons functionality helps you to contend with some of the more competitive sites that demand subscription rates for specific tasks in a classroom.

Nevertheless, you can connect videos at no charge for Google Classroom, and also split them into topics. All the classes, records, applications, and grades are at one convenient location for teachers.

19. Profit From a Simple to Use Device

The classroom of Google can provide highly intuitive, easily learnable lessons. In every stage of the cycle the app talks to you. You'll be invited to "communicate with your class here" when you open the first page of Google Classroom. You can make posts, announcements for scheduled them to go out at a specific time. You can also respond to notices from students. The guide is also self-explanatory, which ensures the application of the app does not have a learning curve.

Teachers provide assignments, and students view them as tasks. Once the work is done it is checked off by the student. A formal collection of job completion measures keeps us focused and tends to prevent uncertainty over the activities that are assigned to them.

Besides the students interacting with each other, the teacher can interact via email with individual students, and even with parents, posts to a stream, private comments, and feedback. Even you may make a class notice that extends to all enrolled students.

You can even sign up as a student if you're an instructor and check how the program functions if you can direct some frustrated students a little. As the environment is more linked, including for topics like graphic design, where students can now access a lesson online and upload research with a whiteboard or attachment, anticipate even further online classes.

20. Ease of Adding New Students

To easily add new learners to Google Classroom you only have to navigate to add "people." You can see a chart of teachers, pupils with a symbol for a little child and a sign for plus on the right. To attach another instructor and you can also share with them your extra workload, or encourage someone to substitute, click on the individual icon next to the word "Teachers."

Students may even attach files to your Google Classroom if you send them the digital code that is located just below the student list.

21. Differentiate Between the Levels of Ability of Students

When you are in a classroom of many ability

levels, with the help of Google Classroom you can distinguish levels by siting up as many specific classrooms as you might want. One example can be self-guided programs of reading. Using the curriculum you can have two to three classes of pupils, like group A is at a 6th grade intellectual level, group B at a 4th grade intellectual level, and group C may be at a 2nd grade intellectual level. With the help of Google Classroom, teachers can split and categorize at their ability level and you can still view all the learners from the same screen to coordinate who's focusing on what. Keeping you up to date on top of who requires extra guidance and who's excelling in the subject and who is struggling.

22. No Excuses

Students, some of them, appear to have a reason for not handing in their assignments forever. You've heard the answer from the old baby threw my homework, but few students make way too many excuses and take them to a new level. Work is given digitally and also always submitted online with a digital classroom, which means it can't be get lost by some random excuse. Digital platforms also let parents stay on top of what their kids have completed and what still needs to be completed.

Many schools often utilize remote instruction on

snow days, rather than requiring students to create cancellations because of bad conditions. Since it would have finished, spring break is no longer split from or school in action for a week later. Alternatively, the school offers links to electronic learning programs, such that even on days when school doesn't, research proceeds.

23. Future Aspect

Google is at the front-line of digital technologies, and it is what electronic services users' desire. An online learning program gives schools and individuals who only want to send others knowledge a chance to do the same without spending too much money. Only free learning software gives you a place to arrange lessons and store records.

Google Classroom restructures the whole schooling cycle by removing the need for documents to be scanned and saved and let you insert grades directly into a scorebook. Alternatively, it all occurs online, eliminating time and better use of energy. Hence, a lot of the time is being saved by Google Classroom and students can concentrate on individual learning.

Conclusion

The most convincing aspect of Google Classroom is that it allows you to interact further outside the school with your pupils. The students at Google Classroom are not needed to be in the classroom physically for them to ask you a question. Students can likewise send research from wherever they have access to the Web. That saves a lot of time for those teachers who teach middle school elective courses when you think about how many students with you can discuss during the school year!

Google Classroom saves you time and paper, and helps you to quickly build courses, post assignments, and interact with students. This also allows you to check-in with the students if they have finished their tasks, so you can give detailed input, ratings in real-time. Essentially, Google Classroom places all of the assignments, updates, and student research in one location.

Any subject you are teaching, Google Classroom is a perfect way to exchange knowledge with your pupils, gather their research, and offer input. If you have a Google account through your district, Google Classroom will just sit there waiting to help you challenge your students and engage them.

The following is a summary of Google Classroom's features:

- Google Classroom brings teachers into touch with students, no matter the distance between them.

- It makes the creation of a class easy and the invitation to learn easier.

- Google Classroom helps instructors to hand out assignments.

- It ensures efficient communication between teachers and students.

- Google Classroom requires making, updating, and labeling tasks for students easier.

- Google Classroom enables students to see assignments in one place, documents, and class materials.

CPSIA information can be obtained
at www.ICGtesting.com
Printed in the USA
BVHW090403080721
611354BV00009B/177